This book is to be returned on or before
the last date stamped below

ALL ABOUT...

THE

Victorians

JANE GOODWIN

Text © Jane Goodwin 2001

Editor: Liz Gogerly

Picture research: Shelley Noronha at Glass Onion Pictures

Inside design: Joyce Chester

Published in Great Britain by Hodder Wayland, an imprint of Hodder Children's Books, in 2001

British Library Cataloguing in Publication Data

Goodwin, Jane

All about the Victorians

1. Great Britain – History – Victoria, 1837–1901 2. Great Britain – Social life and customs – 19th century 3. Great Britain – Politics and government – 1837–1901

I. Title II. The Victorians

941'081

ISBN 0 7502 3602 7

The author and publishers thank the following for permission to reproduce their photographs: Beamish 15 (bottom), 19 (top & bottom), 34 (bottom); Bolton Museum and Art Gallery (title page); Bridgeman Art Library/ Private Collection 15 (top), 25 (top), 27 (bottom), 33 (top), 37 (top), 43 (bottom)/ Crown Estate 7 (top)/ Royal Geographical Society 9 (bottom)/ National Library of Australia 8/ Worshipful Company of Clockmakers' Collection 11 (bottom)/ Phillips, The International Fine Art Auctioneers 11 (top), 30/ Yale Center for British Art, Paul Mellon Collection 14/ Science Museum, London 23 (bottom)/ Victoria and Albert Museum 31 (bottom)/ Hudson Bay Company, Canada 36/ Stapleton Collection, UK 45 (top); Mary Evans 7 (bottom), 13 (bottom), 17, 22, 25 (bottom), 32, 37 (bottom), 39 (bottom), 40 (left & right), 41 (top & bottom), 44, 45 (bottom); Hulton Getty 9 (top), 12; Hodder Wayland Picture Library 13 (top), 20 (top), 38, 41 (bottom); London Transport Board 20 (bottom); Billie Love 23 (top), 27 (top), 28 (bottom), 29 (bottom), 33 (bottom), 39 (top); Manchester Art Gallery (cover); Museum of London 6, 10, 16 (top), 21, 24, 26, 31 (top); National Coal Minining Museum 16 (bottom); Norfolk Museum Services 28 (top), 29 (top); Robert Opie 18, 35 (top & bottom), 42, 43 (bottom)

Please note: We have been unable to trace the copyright holder of *Cecil Rhodes with the Matabeles* (page 43) and would be grateful to receive any information as to their identity.

Printed in Hong Kong by Wing King Tong Co Ltd.

Hodder Children's Books

A division of Hodder Headline Limited

338 Euston Road, London

NW1 3BH

Other titles in the **All About ...** series:

The Coming of the Railways	The First World War	The Great Fire of London
The Great Plague	The Greeks	The Industrial Revolution
The Tudors	The Victorians	

ALL ABOUT...
THE
Victorians

JANE GOODWIN

HODDER
Wayland

an imprint of Hodder Children's Books

Timeline

1819 24 May *Princess Victoria is born.*

1825 *First public railway (Darlington–Stockton) opens.*

1837 *King William IV dies, Victoria becomes queen.*

1838 *Louis Daguerre develops photography in France.*

1840 *Victoria marries her cousin Prince Albert of Saxe-Coburg, Gotha. Penny post is introduced.*

1844 *First Factory Act introduces factory inspectors; dangerous machinery must be fenced.*

1847 *Second Factory Act reduces working day to 10 hours for women and children.*

1851 1 May *Great Exhibition opens.*

1854–1856 *Crimean War, Florence Nightingale establishes field hospitals.*

1857 *Indian Mutiny.*

1867 *Third Factory Act reduces working day to 10 hours for everyone.*

1870 *Education Act creates local Board Schools. Dr Barnardo opens first home.*

1871 *Workers granted four extra bank holidays, trade unions legalized.*

1876 *Alexander Graham Bell invents the telephone in the USA.*

1878 *William Booth starts the Salvation Army.*

1878–1881 *War between Britain and Afghanistan.*

1879 *Edison and Swan develop the electric light bulb.*

1884 *Reform Act gives nearly all men the right to vote.*

1885 *Benz invents the first petrol-engined car in Germany.*

1887 *Queen Victoria celebrates her Golden Jubilee.*

1891 *Education Act makes Board Schools free.*

1897 *Queen Victoria celebrates her Diamond Jubilee.*

1899–1902 *Boer War.*

1901 *Queen Victoria dies on 22 January. Edward VII becomes King.*

CONTENTS

A NEW QUEEN

O n 24 May 1819, Victoria was born. Her father, the Duke of Kent, died soon after. On 20 June 1837 her uncle, King William IV, died and at the age of 18 she became queen. Her prime minister, Lord Melbourne, gave the young queen help and advice on how to rule. She had little real power and any influence she had could only be through the support of her people.

The Coronation of Queen Victoria at Westminster Abbey on 28 June 1838.

This portrait of Victoria in 1843 illustrates a young and confident queen.

In February 1840 she married her cousin Albert. He had a strong sense of public duty and became her most trusted adviser. When he died of typhoid in 1861 she went into deep mourning, and was not seen again in public for many years.

Queen Victoria and Prince Albert with their nine children, four sons and five daughters. The eldest son became King Edward VII.

EMPIRE AND EMIGRATION

During Victoria's reign the area of the world ruled by Britain grew bigger, until it included a quarter of the Earth's population. It was known as the British Empire, and included colonies such as India, Canada, Australia, and in Africa, Kenya and Rhodesia (now Zimbabwe and Zambia). Many people left Britain to help to run these colonies. The unemployed were sent to Australia to find work as it was cheaper than keeping them in the workhouse (see page 26).

A painting of emigrants in search of a new life in Australia.

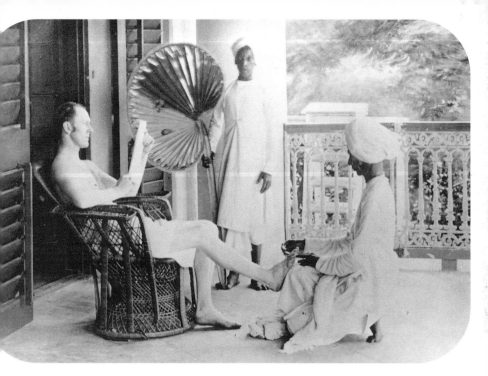

A British army officer is waited upon by local servants in India.

In 1886 the Empire stretched to the five major continents, one fifth of the world's land surface.

In Ireland the potato famine caused widespread starvation and many people emigrated to America. In Scotland the land-owners drove poor people off their land, and these victims of the 'Highland Clearances' also left in hope of a better life.

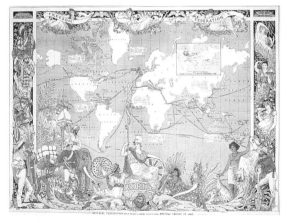

THE GREAT EXHIBITION

The Crystal Palace was built in less than seven months and was designed so that it could be taken down easily when it was no longer needed. Some people even bought season tickets!

O n 1 May 1851 the Great Exhibition opened to the public. It was the idea of Henry Cole, a leading industrialist, who wanted to show that Britain was a great manufacturing and trading nation. Prince Albert liked the idea, and persuaded people to support it. The building that held the exhibition was called the Crystal Palace. It was designed by Joseph Paxton, and was the first building to be made from 'mass-produced' parts.

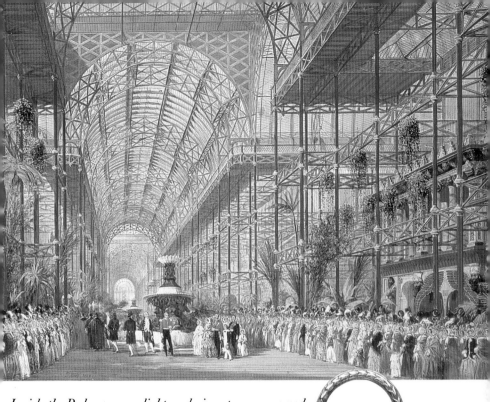

Inside the Palace was a light and airy space crammed with exhibits from Britain and overseas.

It was constructed from glass and iron, and was located in Hyde Park, London. Millions of people went to see the wonderful exhibition of new inventions and goods from all over the world. People travelled by foot, horse-drawn bus, rail and river to get there.

A gold pocket watch made for the Great Exhibition in 1851.

WAR IN THE CRIMEA!

Queen Victoria had a peaceful start to her reign, but in 1853 there was trouble in the Crimea, a peninsula of Russian land in the Black Sea. In 1854 Britain joined her allies France and Turkey in declaring war on Russia. The British Army suffered terrible losses, and many men died before the war ended in 1856. A British nurse called Florence Nightingale travelled to a military hospital at Scutari with a party of female nurses, and took with her medicines, blankets, soap and brushes.

The soldiers had little shelter or warm clothing to protect them from the harsh winter, and not enough food or medicine.

The nurses made sure the hospital was clean and comfortable. In January 1855 nearly half of the wounded soldiers died in hospital, but by June, with proper nursing care, the death rate was down to 2 per cent.

Inside Florence Nightingale's army hospital at Scutari, after she had organized her nursing staff to make it clean and airy.

Mary Seacole, from Jamaica, went to the Crimea to help with the nursing of British soldiers.

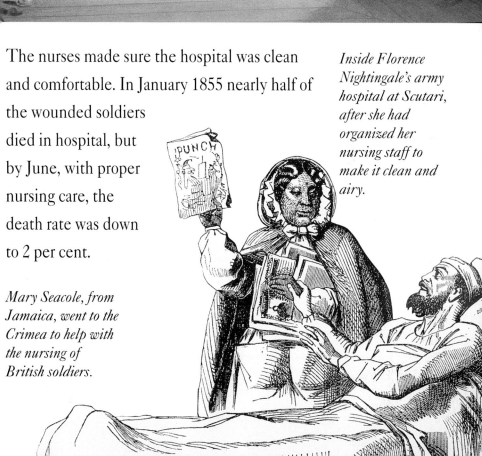

A New Way of Working

Before the Industrial Revolution, most work was done by hand and most people worked on farms. The discovery of steam power and the invention of new machines changed that. Large numbers of machines were gathered together in one building, known as a factory. Flowing water, and later steam, was used to power the whole factory. People moved to the towns to look for work as there were fewer jobs in the countryside.

Inside an ironworks in 1850. The demand increased for iron to build machines, bridges and steam engines.

The new power looms produced cloth quickly, but working conditions were incredibly noisy and dangerous.

Women and young children worked in the factories, and were paid even less than men. The working day was long and hard as people struggled to keep pace with the machines and meet the demands of the factory owners.

In the north of England the large factories were known as mills.

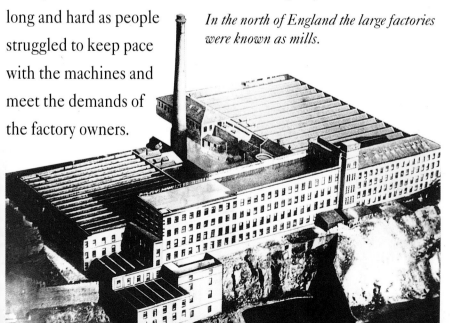

PROTECTING THE WORKERS

From 1833 onwards a number of laws were passed that improved working conditions for women and children. But by 1842 children as young as 3 years of age still worked down coal mines and in factories or were sent up chimneys to sweep them.

By 1875 Lord Shaftesbury had succeeded in getting the use of boys to sweep chimneys made illegal.

The Act of 1844 made it illegal for women and children to work down mines.

By 1844 only children over the age of 8 could work, and between 8 and 13 they also had to have half a day's schooling. Women and older children could only work ten hours a day.

Lord Shaftesbury, a member of the government, was concerned about the welfare of children. He argued for the 1844 Factory Act, which said that dangerous machinery had to be fenced; before that thousands of children were killed and injured by unguarded machines. Another Act in 1847 reduced the working day to ten hours for women and children, and by 1867 all factory workers had a ten-hour day.

FEEDING THE PEOPLE

During Victoria's reign the number of people farming the land halved, even though demand for food was growing. A number of changes took place that made it possible to produce more food. The wet fenland of Norfolk was drained, and turned into good farm land. Science helped farmers to get more out of their farms by rotating crops, and by breeding animals that gave more meat and milk. The light iron plough was used to speed up the cultivation of the soil. Britain also began to import large amounts of grain from the USA.

New machinery allowed farm owners to produce more food, but a lot of farm labourers lost their jobs.

Special animal feeds meant that farm animals produced meat more quickly.

High unemployment in the countryside led to falling wages. Many people left to work in the factories of the growing towns.

Hay making was part of a traditional country life that was changing rapidly.

THE IMPACT OF THE RAILWAYS

George Stephenson developed the steam locomotive from the steam engine built by James Watt. In 1825 the first public railway was built between Darlington and Stockton, followed in 1830 by the Liverpool to Manchester line.

Isambard Kingdom Brunel designed the Great Western Railway that ran from London to Bristol.

After 1846 all railway carriages had to have a roof, so people no longer got covered by soot.

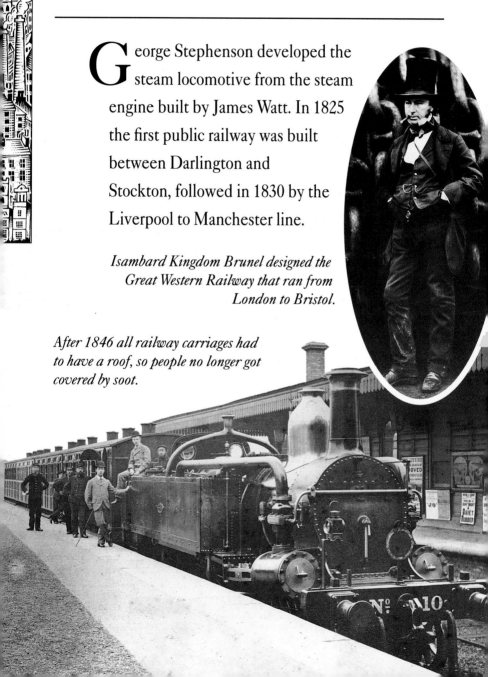

Railway stations, like this one at Charing Cross in London, were always busy as more and more people travelled by rail.

By 1852 most of Britain had access to the rail network. The railways changed the face of Britain. People and goods, such as food, raw materials and letters, travelled more quickly and cheaply than ever before. They provided employment and were used for travel to work, to visit friends and also to go on holiday. Trains helped seaside towns to grow and prosper. Travel was comfortable in first-class compartments, but in the early days third-class travel meant standing in an open carriage.

THE AGE OF INVENTIONS

Factories, railways and machines were changing the way that people worked, but a number of inventions improved everyday life. By 1843 people were able to send telegrams. In 1876 Alexander Graham Bell invented the telephone. Gas was piped to wealthy homes, allowing gas lights and fires to replace coal, candles and oil lamps. Then in 1879 the electric light bulb was developed by two scientists working separately in different countries. Thomas Edison from the USA and Joseph Swan from England eventually joined forces in 1883 to form the Edison and Swan Electric Light Company. Edison also invented the phonograph, which recorded words and music.

Tinned food became more widespread, and people could store food for longer.

Photography was invented in 1839. People had to sit very still for family poses as it took a long time to take a picture.

Hand-operated washing machines, carpet sweepers and sewing machines all made housework a little easier for the middle classes. In 1885 Karl Benz invented the first petrol-engined car.

The telephone used by Queen Victoria at Osborne House. Her calls would be connected by hand at the telephone exchange.

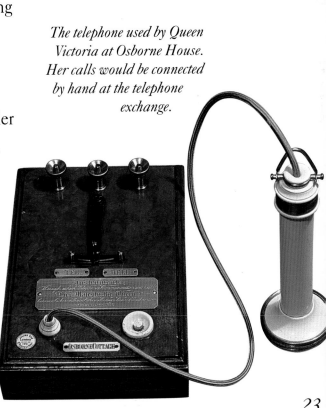

TOWNS GROW BIGGER

In 1800 only a quarter of the British population lived in towns; the figure had reached three-quarters by 1900. London was the biggest city, but the towns that grew in size most quickly were the industrial towns of the north of England, like Manchester, Bradford and Liverpool. People moved there to find work, as there were fewer jobs in the countryside. The factory owners had cheap terraced houses built near to the factories for their workers, but often these crowded areas turned into filthy slums.

Slum housing was over-crowded, with many people living in one room.

With no inside toilets or clean water, diseases spread quickly, and it was impossible to keep clean.

The middle classes also moved to the towns to find employment, as bankers, doctors and businessmen. Their houses were built further out of town, in the new suburbs. These houses were larger, with pleasant gardens, and had indoor toilets and running water.

Every middle-class family had a maidservant, who would be responsible for cleaning and for helping the lady of the house.

LIFE AT HOME

Many working-class families lived in one room, and often shared a bed. Clothes were handed down until they wore out, and few children had shoes or toys. The houses were often built back to back, with shared earth toilets. Life was hard, but it was worse for the homeless. They lived on the streets or in workhouses. Workhouses were built all over the country. These dirty and overcrowded places were usually the only choice for the sick and dying, or young orphaned children.

In a working-class family everyone who could was expected to work. Here the mother and children are making brushes at home.

Middle-class families had a team of servants to look after them and their children.

Life for the middle-classes was much more comfortable. The father was the head of the household, and only he would work. The mother ran the household and organized the servants. The children were often looked after by a nanny. These homes had expensive furniture and carpets. They also had gardens.

Large formal dinner parties, like this Christmas dinner, would be a chance to show how successful you were.

AT SCHOOL

I n early Victorian times there were few schools, but slowly people realized that it was important to educate children. Robert Owen, a mill owner and social reformer, had a school at his factory, and 'ragged schools' were available for poor children. In 1870 the government set up 'board schools'.

A medal presented for good attendance.

A 'board school' was run by a board of governors for local children aged between five and ten years. Boys and girls were taught separately.

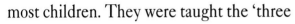

When using your copybook, you had to be careful not to blot it!

From 1891 board schools were free. The school day was quite boring for most children. They were taught the 'three Rs' – reading, (w)riting and (a)rithmetic. They had to chant their times tables, and used copybooks to practise their handwriting. They were taught some history and geography. PE was called 'drill', and while the teacher shouted orders all the children did the same exercise. Classes were big, and teachers often beat the children to keep order.

From 1844 Lord Shaftesbury ran the 'ragged schools' to give some chance of education to the very poorest children.

WOMEN AND CHILDREN

D espite their differences, the one thing rich and poor women had in common was that they were seen as their husband's property. Until 1884 all women had very few rights of their own. Most women had little education. Wealthy girls were taught the skills required to get a 'good husband', such as playing an instrument, and moving gracefully.

Young children were dressed just like their parents, and were expected to be seen and not heard. Good manners were very important.

Clockwork toys made out of tinplate were very popular, like this cart pulled by a zebra.

Rich children would have many different toys, like rocking horses, bricks and board games. For the first time there were books written especially for children. Girls and boys played with different toys – girls would have dolls and a dolls' house, while boys were bought clockwork train sets and lead soldiers. For poor children there were street games that needed little money such as hopscotch, conkers and marbles.

Poor women and children faced a hard life with few pleasures.

ENJOYING YOURSELF

Towards the middle of Victoria's reign, people had more time to enjoy themselves, and sports became very popular. Cricket had been played for many years, but now it was being organized into county matches. Football was popular with working-class people, while rugby was enjoyed by the upper classes. Tennis was one of the few sports that was also popular with women, and they could play alongside men in mixed doubles.

Women played tennis in long skirts and wore hats. By 1884 there was a ladies' singles competition at Wimbledon.

Many books were originally serialized, with a new chapter published every month.

In richer families people learned to play a musical instrument, so they could entertain their friends.

Cycling was enjoyed by those who could afford it. For the middle and upper classes, reading was a popular pastime, and books by authors like Dickens and the Brontë sisters would often be read aloud to the whole family. People enjoyed listening to musical performances and playing board games and cards.

AT THE SEASIDE

Popular songs told of the joys of the seaside.

As working conditions improved, it was possible for people to take holidays or go on day trips to the seaside. In 1871 four extra 'bank holidays' were created. The cheapest and quickest way to get to the seaside was by train. It was a wonderful place to be, away from the smoke-filled air of the industrial towns. People enjoyed the sand and the pier, and even went swimming, although men and women had to change and bathe separately.

People stayed fully dressed on the beach, and used hats to shade themselves from the sun.

Punch and Judy shows were enjoyed as much in Victorian times as they are today.

For children there were donkey rides and fun on the beach. Families would take a big picnic to eat, as there were no cafes. Popular resorts included Brighton, Margate and Blackpool. Queen Victoria enjoyed a day at the seaside too.

People sent postcards to tell their family and friends what a good time they were having.

EXPLORING NEW LANDS

The Victorians were interested in the world, and could travel further and faster than ever before. Many explorers wanted to make new discoveries. John Hanning Speke went to Africa to find the source of the River Nile. Sir John Franklin sailed to the Arctic in search of the North-West Passage between the Atlantic and Pacific oceans. Some, like Dr David Livingstone, wanted to spread Christianity.

Franklin's ships, Terror *and* Erebus, *were caught in the ice in 1845, and everyone died.*

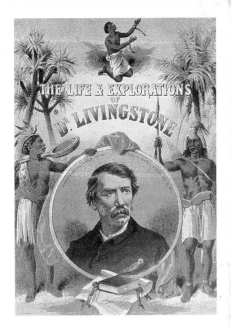

Livingstone explored the Zambezi
river, and crossed Africa from the
Atlantic to the Indian Ocean. He
was the first white man to see the
Victoria Falls. He also gathered
important information about the
local people and products. Other
explorers left Britain to trade and secure new lands.

*British trade relied upon raw materials from all corners
of the Empire.*

MORE RIGHTS FOR THE PEOPLE

I n 1800, only men who owned property were allowed to vote in elections. Between 1867 and 1884 nearly all men won the right to vote in secret ballots, although women had to wait another 44 years for the same rights. From 1834 onwards a number of trade unions were formed. One of the first was the Amalgamated Society of Engineers, which brought together smaller unions of skilled craftspeople. These large unions had more power to improve working conditions for their members. Lord Shaftesbury also introduced laws that reduced working hours and raised the age at which children could work.

On this member's trade union card, Aesop's fable about a bundle of sticks being harder to break than one stick is shown by the kneeling figures

Dr Barnardo worked to help the very poorest people, and in 1870 opened his first 'Home' for homeless children.

The Church was involved in trying to help the homeless and hungry, like this vicar feeding street children.

The Salvation Army was started by William Booth in 1878, and set up soup kitchens and night shelters for the homeless.

"Saved"

VICTORIA – EMPRESS OF INDIA

After Albert's death, Victoria went into deep mourning, and for many years was rarely seen in public. She distrusted Gladstone, the leader of the Liberal Party, but was a close friend of Disraeli, who created for her the title Empress of India. With his guidance, Victoria was seen in public more often. In 1887 she celebrated her Golden Jubilee, which meant she had ruled for 50 years. She travelled to a service in Westminster Abbey through cheering crowds.

The Diamond Jubilee was celebrated with a special issue of the Penny Illustrated Paper.

Benjamin Disraeli, a very ambitious man, was the Conservative Prime Minister *twice.*

*Victoria was delighted with her title
Empress of India, and said that
India was 'the Jewel in my crown'.*

In 1897 her Diamond Jubilee (to celebrate 60 years as queen) attracted even bigger crowds, and she rode through London with 50,000 troops from all over the Empire. The Empire was at its greatest, and people were proud of the wealth and importance that it brought. Trouble, however, lay ahead.

*People could buy
souvenirs for both
jubilees. This
special cup and
saucer commemorate
the Diamond
Jubilee of 1897.*

THE BOER WAR

A s time went on, there were an increasing number of conflicts in the Empire. The biggest overseas war started in South Africa in 1899, and is called the Boer War. It was fought between Britain and the Boers, the descendants of Dutch settlers who controlled large areas of Southern Africa. When gold was discovered in those areas, Britain wanted a share. The British claim was supported by Cecil Rhodes, who believed that the British should rule Africa. At first, the Boers were successful but they couldn't hold out against a growing British army. With nearly half a million British soldiers in South Africa, the Boers eventually lost in 1902.

The British victory was celebrated on packaging, like this Bovril label showing the British flag flying over South Africa.

Defenders of our Empire

THE ORIGINAL SAMUEL ALLEN'S EMPIRE CHOCOLATE MANUFACTURED IN LONDON

There were conflicts in India, Afghanistan, New Zealand, Jamaica and Africa. Britain needed a large army.

Many people were unhappy that Britain had gone to war against another country. Others were concerned about the cost in lives and money. Support for the Empire began to weaken.

Cecil Rhodes was a businessman who became the Prime Minister of Cape Colony. He eventually founded Rhodesia, now Zimbabwe and Zambia.

THE END OF AN ERA

Victoria's death on 22 January 1901, aged 81 ended the longest reign in British history, and 63 years of great change. Most people now lived in towns, where Boards of Health made sure people had clean drinking water and proper sewage treatment. Children had a right to basic education, and most men could vote. Railways connected the whole country. Although a third of Londoners still lived in poverty, there was a desire to improve living conditions for everyone.

Victoria, with her successors, Edward VII top right, George V bottom left and Edward VIII as a baby.

Huge crowds attended the funeral procession of the Queen.

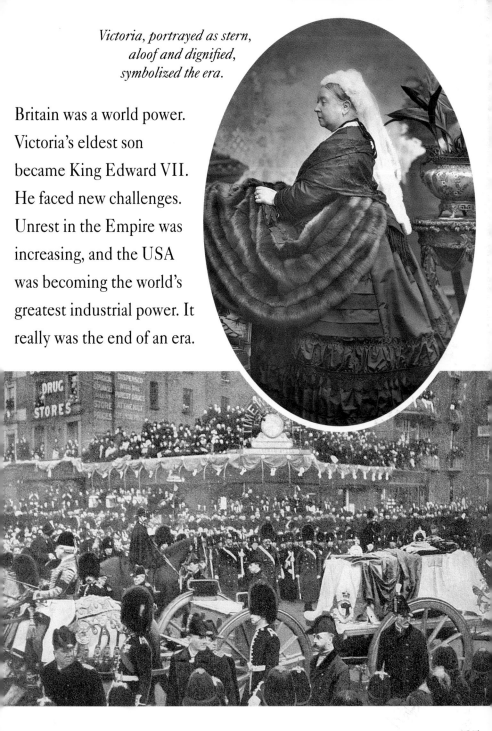

Victoria, portrayed as stern, aloof and dignified, symbolized the era.

Britain was a world power. Victoria's eldest son became King Edward VII. He faced new challenges. Unrest in the Empire was increasing, and the USA was becoming the world's greatest industrial power. It really was the end of an era.

GLOSSARY

bank holiday *A public holiday, created by parliament, originally the only weekdays on which banks closed.*

Cape Colony *The area of South Africa under British rule.*

coronation *The ceremony at which a king or queen is crowned.*

crop rotation *The practice of planting crops in three fields and leaving one field as grass so the soil can recover. The unplanted field is changed every year. Rotation over four fields was introduced in the eighteenth century.*

earth toilet *A toilet that has a wooden seat over a ditch.*

empire *Different lands all ruled over by one country.*

emigrate *To move to another country and become a citizen of that country.*

fenland *An area of low marshy land in Norfolk.*

Highland Clearances *When small scale farmers were driven off the land by the owners of large country estates.*

import *To bring in goods from another country.*

jubilee *A celebration of something that has lasted a number of years – a golden jubilee is for 50 years, and a diamond jubilee is for 60 years.*

mass-produced *Made in large numbers by mechanical methods.*

peninsula *A piece of land that is surrounded by water on three sides.*

potato famine *Most people in Ireland depended on potatoes for food; when the crop failed there was widespread starvation.*

secret ballot *A vote cast in private.*

serialized *A story which is told in a number of instalments – like episodes of a television drama.*

telegram *A message sent over a distance using electrical impulses.*

trade *To carry on business by exchanging products, usually for money.*

typhoid *An infectious disease that causes fever and sickness, and often results in death.*

weaving loom *A machine that turns thread into fabric.*

workhouse *A place where those without jobs could find shelter and food. Families were broken up there and the workhouse was widely feared and hated.*

INDEX